COVID
almost
killed the
CEO

How a near-death experience
birthed a new life

Dan Thompson

FREILING
PUBLISHING

Published by Freiling Publishing,
a division of Freiling Agency, LLC.

P.O. Box 1264
Warrenton, VA 20188

www.FreilingPublishing.com

ISBN: 978-1-956267-16-7

Printed in the United States of America

Dedication

THIS BOOK IS dedicated to my wife Nicole; my daughters Taylor, Shelby, and Haiden; and my sons Seth and Drew.

Thank you to all of you who gave me thoughts and prayers during my battle with COVID-19.

Thank you to the higher power of God for the miracle of life and for giving me a second chance. Thank you to my parents for life itself and for listening to me daily following my COVID-19 experience.

This is further dedicated to my mother-in-law Rosemary, father-in-law Kent, and brother-in-law Jon, all of whom sadly passed away all too early in the last six years.

During the writing of this book, I also dedicate this to my father, who died from a horrible battle with lung cancer on May 30, 2021.

Table of Contents

Foreword

To the families who have lost loved ones from this terrible pandemic, my thoughts and prayers to you. To the healthcare workers who perform the work necessary to implement life-saving protocols, I am grateful for your work. I am proud of every healthcare worker from physician, nurse, and nutritionist to those in housekeeping. Thank you to all of the essential workers who fearlessly work endless hours to assist the COVID-19 patients and their families. Humankind is working together to protect humankind from the unknown.

As it's been said all across our country and worldwide, the year 2020 brought us one of the biggest challenges that we will never forget. It has thrown us all off balance, both physically and mentally. Mental illness was already a growing problem in our country, and yet the pandemic has amplified the problem of mental illness even more. As they say, COVID brain is a condition caused by COVID-19; however, there isn't much said about people's experiences with it. I hope you enjoy my story.

My thoughts are with the families of children who have lost their lives to COVID-19 as well as the children who have lost their ability to be heard while hidden behind COVID-19 masks. My kids went through the school year with masks on. As a teacher put it best, it's hard to read the faces of children whom I cannot see.

Teachers play such an important part of identifying children who appear to be sad, or children who seem to be confused about a question. Seeing only the eyes of students makes it very hard to teach.

Let us all pray for an end of this pandemic and hope that widespread "herd immunity" will occur once the majority of the population receives a vaccine. Thank you to the medical science community and the regulators who acted swiftly in bringing the vaccines forward quickly to the masses.

Let's hope that the summer of 2021 brings us back together on vacations and that a growing number of Americans gets vaccinated. This will make our country more confident, and we will see a massive growth in economic prosperity into 2022.

Our family suffered the enormous tragedy of losing a father-in-law, mother-in-law, and brother-in-law, all in a six-year period. My wife is the last one left in her family. I never thought that after seventeen years of marriage, our entire world would disappear. My in-laws were only in their early seventies. My brother-in-law, in his early forties, unfortunately passed away from a losing battle to opioid addiction. The pandemic happened right after that. It couldn't have come at a tougher time for us while we were grieving from the loss of family members who were so important to us.

But we made it through, thanks to the powers that be and the strength of love for each other.

1

Humble Beginnings

I T WAS FEBRUARY 2, 1978. I was the first son and the first grandchild born into a large family. My mother's side was all Catholic. My father had converted from Presbyterian. It was a prerequisite that he convert to Catholicism for him to marry my mother. I think my Irish Catholic grandmother would not have allowed the marriage to happen otherwise. She was tough like that. In addition to that fact, my dad is older than my mother by eleven years. I am sure that bugged my grandmother a bit also. My dad bought my mother a late 1970s convertible Camaro in 1977 and they drove across the U.S. together. They were very much in love.

I remember one summer in the nineties when we were in Ocean City, Maryland. The waves were an attractive height for surfing, and it was a beautiful day. My mom was sunbathing in a bikini, and my dad was in his construction-themed trucker-looking hat and dark sunglasses with a farmer's tan, complete with a dark mustache and overgrown sideburns. He probably didn't want to be on the beach, but he was there for Mom, sitting in a cheap folding chair off to the side. All of a sudden, a surfer ran up, planted his surfboard near my mom, and said to my dad, "Hey, sir, do you mind if I take your daughter out to show her surfing?" That was a funny moment even for me at a young age. I got it right away. I don't think my dad was as humored.

My mother was the oldest of four, the other three being all boys, and they were all delighted to have a nephew to play with. It was a pretty cool situation, especially since I had grandparents on both sides, even great-grandparents, all of whom contributed to a wonderful upbringing. Cherished values and inspiration—those were wonderful times. I hardly remember the beginning because I was so little, but as the years went on, I started accumulating the memories.

I was followed by a sister and brother, each of us two years apart. Then my parents had another daughter; I was thirteen at the time. My mother dealt with two pre-teens, one teenager, and one infant. By the mid-1990s we had moved to the tiny town of Salisbury, Maryland. I was now in public school, and my siblings were in a private school. I remember one evening my parents put all of us in the dining room for dinner. It wasn't a specific holiday or any special occasion, for that matter. In the middle of the dining room table was a book, what seemed to be a middle school or high school yearbook. This was the day that my parents announced to us that we had another sibling, an older brother, from my dad's first marriage, which none of us knew about. It was an interesting surprise. The sister that is closest to my age took this as an opportunity to meet him. She literally hunted him down and brought him to meet us. He and my dad reconciled after decades of being absent from one another. I guess you could call it burying the hatchet. I guess you could also say we are one big super complicated nuclear family.

I describe my childhood as a paradoxical upbringing. People say that how you are raised is how your whole life is shaped. Your exposure as a child and the experiences you have as a kid are all what mold you into an adult. I never really appreciated it then as a kid, which makes sense.

My father's mother was a self-made school teacher. She began her career in a one-room schoolhouse at the age of sixteen. She raised my dad and his brother herself. She had a divorce when the boys were young, but she successfully brought up both my dad and uncle.

My grandfather died before I was born. Although he had left my grandmother, he was a West Point graduate, and he had dozens of patents. He was in World War II, stationed all over the Pacific. He saw massive action and had been awarded the Purple Heart. He invented the first self-sharpening lawn mower, which he sold to Sears in the 1960s.

My grandmother was tremendously successful for a school teacher who didn't have major financial resources. I spent many weekends with her as a kid. At the time, I was upset to go there because she made me write sentences. She had large-lined sheets of paper, like presentation-size sheets that folded over. I had to write words and tell her their meanings. I had to do math. I had to read and tell her about the reading. By the time I was almost an early teenager, I spent weekends with her grading the high school papers with her. Maybe that was her plan when I was younger. The academic instruction from her and the education from the private school were huge contributions to my life.

One of my memories with my grandmother was when I woke up one morning and wanted breakfast. She told me to go make it myself, and I did, although it was the first time I ever made scrambled eggs on a gas stove. She also asked me to go in the scary basement to light a large furnace by myself. I remember opening the old door in the kitchen and looking down into a dark, dirt-floor basement. Each stair creaked and squeaked as I made my way down to the furnace. That was one of the scariest moments of my life. I think she wanted me to learn survival skills early on.

I also remember the exact day that this grandmother died from a sudden aneurysm. When we got the call, I felt as if my heart had been ripped out. I always keep a picture of Grandmother Thompson by my bedside table. She's always been with me, and she was an incredible inspiration in my life.

On the other end of the spectrum was my mother's side of the family. My grandparents were wealthier, married, and raised four children together. My grandmother was the family protector, the chief Irish Catholic family connector. My grandfather was brilliant. He had the mind of an engineer. He worked many jobs raising the kids and family in New York—Long Island to be specific. He was the classic Italian guy. He was also a navy guy. He spent months out on diesel submarine missions while my grandmother raised the kids at home.

My grandfather even had a career with NASA at one point and worked on the lunar landing module project.

My uncles tell me that his name is on a plaque that is on the moon. Our family still has the blueprints and many autographed pictures of astronauts from the old NASA days.

My stays with these grandparents consisted of watching movies, eating ice cream, visiting toy stores, spending time with uncles, playing pool, and swimming in the pool behind the house. When my parents came to pick me up, I usually hid and didn't want to go with them.

These grandparents were an incredible part of my life. They moved to Florida where we moved in the year 2000. My grandmother unfortunately passed away, having suffered from cancer. My grandfather died of pulmonary fibrosis. Both were tragic and devastating losses for our family. Even to this day, we all miss them. Both of my grandparents are beautifully buried together in a memorial wall at St. Agnes Catholic Church, here in Naples, Florida. For years I always wanted to visit them following the memorial services and celebration of their lives.

It was before 7:00 A.M., and the bus had just picked me up from our middle-class neighborhood in Olney, Maryland. I was about ten years old and in the fifth grade. I was dressed in a black slacks, white dress shirt, clip-on tie, shiny dress shoes, vest, and super-heavy backpack. The bus not only picked up the St. Peter's Catholic School children, but it also picked up the public school kids. The private school kids were outnumbered 15 to 1, and only one bus driver meant that we were going to be under attack for most of the ride. Our destination was a large public school where the private school kids would get out of the bus first and line up against the red brick wall along the school. We would watch the public school kids go into the school. Then we would file back into the bus to be driven to the Catholic school. It was a humiliating way to start every school day, and I did it for years along with many other kids. The best part was when the public school kids made fun of our uniforms or pulled our ties off. Or better yet, when they grabbed our backpacks or took out items. The ride from the public school back to the private school was really the most peaceful time and the quietest. You must be thinking, what would the bus driver do? The roads were pretty treacherous, especially in the winter months, when the driver was focused on driving. There wasn't much the driver could do; it wasn't in the job description to be a babysitter. They say what doesn't kill you makes you stronger.

My dad was in the construction business during the 1980s, and Mom was a homemaker. Dad was a Vietnam veteran, Twenty-fifth Infantry Division, U.S. Army. He was very proud of his Bronze Star. And if you are willing to listen, he would tell you about it, as he was blessed with the gift of gab. He attributed his life, specifically the Vietnam part, as terrible luck when his number was pulled during the draft. But he proudly served his country.

Dad arrived in Vietnam expecting the worst. He didn't have any real expectation of what the country looked like, how it was going to be, or what would happen in terms of war. It wasn't long after he arrived in Vietnam that he was pulled aside and asked to embark on a different mission. He was asked to use a 35-mm SLR film camera to take photos of body parts that came into the headquarters. As he described it, there were thousands of soldiers in Vietnam who died from friendly fire, suicide, drug overdose, or mental insanity. My father typed letters to the families proclaiming that they died in honor, in battle, for our freedom. In some sense they died in a foreign country, miserable. In the end, somehow, this was justified. I think this burned my father's soul his whole life. The Bronze Star that he was awarded wasn't enough for him to bury the reality of his task. When he arrived back to the states, he faced a divorce and lost custody of his first son, whom he didn't see for twenty-plus years. He never told us the real story about Vietnam until weeks before his death from lung cancer.

During the 1980s in our family, Dad worked tirelessly doing what he thought was the best way to raise a family. He hustled in the construction business, paying bills that were much larger than his budget, including paying for three kids to go to Catholic school. I think he was trying to make my Irish Catholic grandmother happy—after all, he converted to Catholicism before he could marry my mother. As they say, timing is everything, though his world came crashing down with the recessionary period during the 1980s. You could say we lost it all. And to top it off, my father lost his mother to that fatal aneurysm. I remember standing in my parents' project house in Showell, Maryland when the news came about my grandmother. It was a horrible day for everyone.

As I finish writing this book, it's Memorial Day, May 31, 2021. My father passed away yesterday. He sadly lost his fight with cancer, which most likely started in the lungs. Dad had been a lifelong smoker. It seemed that one minute we were texting and talking, and the next minute we had a priest coming into hospice to declare Dad's final proper passage. It wasn't but an hour later that he passed into the hands of the Lord. Love you, Dad. I am grateful that I was able to help my siblings all put their judgment at the cross prior to Dad's passage. I will never forget that I accomplished this with incredible dignity and peace. I feel that my dad passed knowing that all of his children loved him to the very last second.

It was the early nineties. My parents had a beach house in Ocean City, Maryland. My dad said to me, "Son, if you want to eventually pay for your own car and insurance, you need to start working." I think I was fourteen or fifteen. So I started working at a beach stand renting umbrellas and boogie boards. I also scooped softballs at a batting cage with a wide shovel in nearly 100-degree weather.

As a family, each summer we would pose on the beach for the famous beach Telescope Pictures photographer. If you don't know about this, telescope pictures were a big thing in the 1990s and still are today. The history of telescope pictures goes back to the 1950s. Essentially, they are photos in a tiny viewfinder with a little chain attached to it. You have to hold it up to the light to see the photo. In Ocean City, there was a monopoly for years with one studio. Eventually the city stopped the monopoly and granted room for one competitor. So for the coastal town of Ocean City, there were two companies selling telescope pictures. The photographers had the best job in the world; they ran up and down the beaches shooting photos on manual Olympus cameras, and assistants were running alongside to grab the film canisters. Meanwhile the photographers were posing families, spring breakers, you name it. They were trained to do professional poses, pyramids, stacking, hand on hip, muscle man, and many more. The key was finding a big family and shooting hundreds of pictures, giving the family a ticket to visit the store downtown at night after a long beach day. It became a family pastime to pose for pictures on the beach during the day and then go to dinner, all cleaned up, and afterward go to the studio to look at the day's beach pictures. By evening, the photographer had cleaned up professionally and greeted the customers at the studio who were captured on film during the day. Once Grandma and Mom grabbed the telescopes and saw the smiling, laughing kids or families in the photos, they were sold. You could say that the telescope picture photographers were celebrities on the beach. I remembered these guys and gals when I was very little, and it was a dream of mine to become one of them.

It was the mid-1990s, and I was looking for other jobs I wanted to do. I still had the burn and itch to be a telescope picture photographer, so I drove out to Ocean City. We had recently moved from the Baltimore/Washington area to Salisbury, and it was only another 30 minutes to Ocean City. If I were going to work as a telescope picture photographer, I had a 30- to 45-minute drive out to the coastal town of Ocean City. I couldn't be the party guy who lived in Ocean City. I went and applied. I met the owner/manager of the telescope picture company. They hired me and helped me pursue my dreams of becoming a telescope picture photographer on the beach. For weeks prior to summer starting, they trained us new hires every day on the beach on all of the poses, how to sell the customer, how to use the camera, how to develop the film, the pitch, and the sales process. I got up every day and never missed a single day, arriving on the beach by 7:00 A.M., and drove home late at night. I felt that I was ready. I was even issued an official Telescope Pictures shorts and t-shirt. I could visualize thousands of people on the beach who were ready to be photographed, ready to be posed in the format I had been trained for. I was ready to hit it and do my dream job.

The manager/owner lined up all the trainees just days before season was to start. He had something to tell us. He said that the veteran photographers were all returning and that we, the trainees, were going to be working in the studio only, sweeping, cleaning, and developing film. We would make only hourly pay. All of the other trainees were grateful and willingly accepted defeat. But I stood up to the manager/owner and told him I quit. I told him that it was unfair to promise all of us the job, only to be smashed down to a studio hourly job. His opinion was that we had to work for the summer as trainees and then maybe the following year, we would obtain a territory. I was probably 16 years old and had enough. I took off my Telescope Pictures shirt, left it on the counter, and walked across the street to the competitor. I walked in the door and asked for the owner/manager. He willingly spoke with me immediately. He hired me right on the spot after I told him what went down. I proceeded to kick the ass of all the veterans who worked for the competitor that trained me. I got to my beach every day at 7:00 A.M. and photographed all of the moms and babies. Once my competitor showed up at the beach, most of the people had already gotten photos from me, so my competitor had nothing to shoot. That was one of my most memorable times of my life. Never give up, never give in, and never ever quit. Do what your gut tells you is right. I would live by this in all of my decisions in life, both personally and professionally.

Fast forward to the late 1990s when my parents were looking for a new start. My uncle on my mother's side and his wife decided to make Naples, Florida, a permanent home. My uncle started to convince my mother that Naples was the place to be. He didn't have to convince her anymore after she visited. She never looked back. My entire family moved to Florida just as I was finishing my undergraduate work. I had choices to make, and I decided I'd rather be with family and move to Florida with them. I was 21 years old and had some ideas of my own.

In 2001, as I was finishing my master's degree in south Florida, I was also running my own photography business. I wanted to digitize wedding photography and did many weddings. I remember them all. I marketed myself to country clubs, hotels—anywhere I could get a good lead. Needless to say, I was busy on the weekends, shooting weddings, editing photos, and selling the packages. I used a digital process that I created with printers that automatically printed photos.

One of my favorite memories is when I talked a small city into letting me shoot a Santa and Mrs. Claus event in its public park. I recruited little people as elves, built a fake gingerbread house, and set up candy canes as markers for people to line up. It was one of the first times that my wife Nicole went to a photo job with me. Hundreds of kids and families showed up and waited patiently. All of the machines were ready to print photos. Everyone was in position. The traditional roaring siren classic fire engine rolled into the park, and everyone cheered. As Santa and Mrs. Claus approached the seating area nestled in the gingerbread house, the children were smiling ear to ear. Suddenly, the public park power went out, and we went immediately to absolute darkness. Luckily, in a matter of minutes, the local municipality utility workers appeared on the scene and fixed the problem, and we were back up and running. We literally shot pictures of kids on Santa's lap for six hours straight. It was very rewarding, stressful, and another learning moment, but I pulled it off.

During the week I worked as a pharmacy tech at a local pharmacy chain and also worked in sales. My first real sales job was working for Gateway Computers. Remember the cow pattern boxes? My job was to upsell add-on software or even hardware including cameras. Nobody could ever sell as many computers as I could in a day.

One day, all of the sales team gathered around in what appeared to be a farm silo (themed like the Dakotas, home of Gateway). Gateway Computers had thousands of people who had gone online to the website and applied for credit. They had previously been denied due to their lousy credit scores. For some reason, the company was willing to take on these people who had been declined. I looked at that list like it was gold. I was shown how to make the calls, get people on the phone, and talk them back into these credit card options to buy a computer.

They could have the entire computer system, software upgrades, and hardware upgrades for as little as $29 per month, basically for the rest of their lives. I think my best day at Gateway Computers was close to thirty full computer systems sold, but most days it was twelve to fifteen in a day. They gave me the list of people in Guam, and I sometimes stayed overnight dialing the phones and making sales, all while everyone else slept. Some of the people I worked with thought I oversold people on computers and accessories.

I remember a certain customer who was a grand-mother. She was excited to have her grandchildren over who never had a computer before. I think I sold her every CD program and every accessory such as a gaming console, a camera system, you name it. I did feel like I had sold her down a river, but she actually wrote me a letter personally to tell me about how her grandchil-dren enjoyed their summer so much because of the new computer. She even sent me some pictures of her and her grandkids with it. If you sell with heart and do it for the right purpose, it always pays back dividends.

I moved out of my parents' place while I was starting grad school, as I was easily able to pay for my own place given the amount of work I was doing. At this point, I had taken my sales experience from Gateway and my desire to do things on my own (photography) to pursue my dreams of being in pharmaceutical sales. I initially took a few interviews with pharmaceutical companies, but they all wanted outside sales experience. I ended up initially working for Paychex payroll company, which was a great experience. I had an incredible sales mentor named

Nancy Miller. She was an amazing leader, inspirer, and doer. She made things happen that nobody else could, and everyone loved her. She pulled me into a sales team that was made up of veterans in one office and helped me ease into the role. I felt so comfortable with her that she became a super friend and mentor. She did everything with heart and true meaning. And I was honest with her that my real goal was to go onto pharmaceutical sales. She helped me achieve goals and build the outside sales experience I needed at the time. It was a phenomenal nearly two years with Paychex before I moved onto what I thought would be my dream job. I've always wondered how Nancy Miller is and I always wanted to thank her for the gifts she instilled in me.

I drafted a solid résumé and started searching for this dream job. I had many interviews and was selected by a foreign-based pharmaceutical company. I had no idea what I was doing or who I was going to work for; I just wanted "the job." Many young people probably fall victim to this just because they don't stop and ask questions. Regardless, I was destined to try this field. So there I was representing anti-spasmodic drugs and anti-hypertensive drugs, and I was going through training. I had to travel far to learn the pharmaceutical language. All we really learned was the psychology behind selling doctors. The successful pharmaceutical rep was one who could convince doctors and get them hooked on writing lots of prescriptions for our products. At training we got to hear the "king" of this particular company talk about how he convinced hundreds of doctors to write prescriptions for these particular drugs. He was the envy of everyone. He even had a PowerPoint presentation just about himself and the Mercedes that the company had purchased for him as a gift. I actually rode in the taxi with him from the airport. He was nice guy in a super sharp suit and nice watch who knew how to convince people to do things. In hindsight, I actually think he was a lousy sales guy.

After the training, I was given my territory, which covered over a several hundred–mile radius. I visited doctors in the early 2000s when it was less regulated than it is today. I remember distinctly that doctors would demand we pay for lunches for nurses or demand specific things to get them to write prescriptions for the medications.

On one such visit, I went to see a certain doctor who had never written orders for our company's products. I was told not to visit with him, but I wanted to see if I could turn his opinion around. When I visited him, he gave me two minutes to tell me he would never write prescriptions for my company's products. I pushed him to find out why. He escorted me to the medicine sample cabinet, which looked like a spare bedroom closet with flimsy doors that slide open on rails from the middle out to the sides. The doctor opened the doors and said, "You see, your products are all alphabetized at the bottom; therefore, I won't be bending down to grab those."

I learned so much about the pharmaceutical business every day. While I did remarkably well, the company I worked for kept hazing us with more requirements, more sales tactics, and more demands to spend money, all to convince doctors to keep writing.

I remember the line I had to memorize: "Dr. XXX, would you write product X for the next twenty-five patients with hypertension who walk through your door, and if you do, I will pay for lunches for the next six months for your staff." I would also post an ad to recruit nursing staff for them, with lunch provided. I do have to add a disclaimer that not all doctors are crooks; most them were great to their patients and truly wrote prescriptions that were necessary. But with others, it was all self-interest and self-enrichment, not the interest of the patients, which was saddening.

Doing my dream career started to eat at my soul because I was also helping take care of my great aunt, and she was on an excessive amount of medications. One of her doctors was on my route. I asked him about my aunt specifically. He took her off of four medications that he was writing purely for gains rather than for her health and wellness. That never sat with me right. And I thought of the thousands of people who probably were on the same excessive pill schedules.

The straw that broke the camel's back for me with pharmaceuticals was a particular manager. He was the fifth manager I had in a twelve-month period. My morning routine was to load up my car with samples for various products and head out on my route. I had specific writers who I supported by detailing them with product information, often reminders about our products. I would fit in the occasional new suspect and pop into the local or national pharmacy to see the pharmacists. It was actually more fun to talk with pharmacists because they were much less stressed. On this particular day, the new manager called me. He said he was going to ride with me on my route. There is nothing more nerve-racking than a manager breathing down my neck when I was already producing, doing my job, and making the company a fortune.

I packed up my old Ford Taurus sedan with pharmaceutical samples and waited for the manager to arrive. He arrived late and then told me we'd better get moving. The whole time this guy never shut up; it was completely annoying. But I tolerated it. He told me stories about how his career was so important and how having him with me would make the doctors write even more scripts. He was all about money, power, and zero meaning. At our second stop, the doctor was really tough. The physician and her team were very specific about procedure. It had taken me nearly a year just to build rapport and to start getting her to write prescriptions for our products. The office was comfortable with me. I knew something was bound to go wrong.

We walked into this particular practice, greeted by the same front desk team. They looked at me and gave the proverbial "nod" to go back and wait for the doctor. Not everyone got the "nod." The manager waltzed in right behind me. Rule #1 of pharmaceutical sales is detailing at the right time, not speaking out of turn, and never kicking up random conversations with patients. This manager did it all wrong. He began loud conversations with the patients in the waiting room. He was massively impatient while we respectfully waited for the doctor to finish with her last patient and see us. You could tell the doctor was mad, the staff was mad, and the patients were all annoyed.

I remember the second when my work was completely destroyed building rapport with the doctor, and she would never write a medication in my bag, ever again. The icing on the cake was when the doctor finally emerged, walking toward us in the hallway. The manager burst out loud and said to the doctor, "Are you Jewish?"

I wanted my head to slide down into my dress shirt and away forever. The doctor replied, "No, why do you ask?"

The manager remarked, "I thought you looked like it." We were invited to leave immediately.

Now, since the manager was my boss, I was personally insulted that the company I represented would put a guy like this through. It was horrifying. The silver lining was that the day did get better until the very moment he was driving away and I never had to see him again.

After almost a full year in pharmaceuticals, my dream job wasn't a dream job. It was a nightmare. I didn't see a future for me. I knew payroll, though. So I ran back to payroll. It was all I knew and all I was comfortable with. The only problem was that my old job was given away at Paychex and I had no choice but to stay in Naples, Florida, with my new wife and newborn baby. I gave my resignation letter to the pharmaceutical industry and signed on with another payroll company.

2

Entrepreneurial Journey Continues

FINISHED MY UNDERGRAD work at University of Maryland in the year 2000 in business administration. I spent part of the time at the business school and part of my time at the philosophy house, reading very rich content and books about philosophical greats such as Socrates, Plato, Aristotle, Tolstoy, and many others.

I really loved the philosophy house at Salisbury State University. Every college student needs to experience advanced philosophy. The courses were awesome. They consisted of reading the great philosophers and then hours of talking about them in sort of a Socratic method. The expansion of the mind was priceless and it opened my thoughts to infinite creativity. I recently donated to the now Salisbury University. The Alumni Association student volunteer that called asked me about my experiences in college and I told her about the philosophy house. She will be electing coursework there, and I guaranteed her it would expand her mind and view on the world. I love inspiring and helping others.

On the other hand, I really enjoyed business school. I spent a tremendous amount of time with my fellow business school friends on various projects on financial management, among other things. A few friends of mine and I started a webpage building company. We even had crazy ideas to call on local businesses in the late 1990s and encourage them to get a webpage. I think we built webpages for about five companies. It was about the process more for us than the money. We met once a week and wrote HTML code. The band of IT geeks eventually broke up, mostly due to other interests (especially girls), but it was truly a cool feeling to know we could start something and make it work. At the time, my dad worked for an architectural and engineering company. He introduced me to the partner of the company. Web-builders built their very first website. Maybe if we stuck with it, it would be the Apple of today.

My parents announced their move to Florida just following my college graduation. I could have stayed in Maryland, but I decided to go to Florida to be with family. I would pursue my MBA in Florida, which I accomplished. It was the best move I ever made, though I didn't realize it at the time. Family above all is the most important thing to me—more than money, and more than anything material. I love my siblings and parents incredibly.

With some courage, I got into my Mazda pickup after loading all of my belongings into the back. A fresh tarp strapped everything down. I made the journey from Maryland to Florida, which was almost a 20-hour drive. I really had no expectation of what I would see, how my life would go, or even what Naples, Florida, was all about. I remember turning down Airport Pulling Road, wondering if this was the right choice for me. I pulled into the parking lot of the hotel where my parents were temporarily staying while the Naples house was being built. I get out of the truck to stretch, went around to the back, and saw the bungee cord over the tarp had been rubbing its way through onto the new paint, now exposing bare metal on the outside of the tail gate. Mind you, I had worked very hard for this truck. The good news was I made it safe to Florida, with an entirely open opportunity to figure out my next move.

It takes time for people to find their stride, as they say. I had the photography business building up. I continued to do weddings and special events, making enough money to support my growing family. I pushed hard toward the dream of pharmaceutical sales. I was young, chasing dreams, making things happen, and trying to find purpose. But pharma sales wasn't it. I didn't see a purpose in pushing pills. I still loved photography, not the money, but the feeling, the emotions driven by the moments I captured and the very lives I impacted. It was photography that led me to my next professional adventure, which would lead me to my passion of helping people.

I had taken a photography job for a local insurance agency. I shot portrait pictures for executives, sales people, and operations people. I provided the images on CD. The leadership was incredibly welcoming—they were friendly, enjoyable people. There was one person who was a VP of sales. He would later become a deeply close friend and long-time mentor. He was committed to doing what was right for the company, which was exactly what he was there to do. He always felt compelled to follow what the CEO said to do. I admire him for that. As most people say in the insurance industry, I kind of fell into insurance. Nobody really gets recruited into it, and in insurance sales, the turnover for insurance producers is usually 75 percent or more because not many people can hack it. For me, it's in my DNA.

After a short few years in the payroll industry building up top sales accolades and still taking pictures professionally, I made the shift to the insurance business. I fell into it after doing those headshots and was abruptly inserted into unemployment from my last payroll company. You can say I was fired. You have to go through failures to achieve successes.

This is a particularly good story related to success and failure. As a consultant I once met said, you have to go to the bottom to get to the top, like climbing Mount Everest, descending after each ascent, slowly making it to the summit.

I was crushing it at a very large national payroll company. I had worked at one service provider, left on good terms to enter the pharma business, and then ran back to the payroll business, only to find my territory gone. So I went to the other service provider, who gladly made me an offer. I also became the top sales guy there. The story part isn't that tumultuous roller coaster ride; it was the end part. So picture this: I took my wife to Paris and London for the prestigious President's Club, we were swept off to lavish excursions, food, and tours—the best of the best. We arrived back to our home following the best trip of our lives.

I returned to my office within a few days of the trip and was called in to meet with the sales leadership guys. Back then, we didn't have much in the way of internet ads, and the twenty-first century dependency on smart phones wasn't quite here yet, so we had the yellow pages—a printed book that was the all-encompassing source of information. They were everywhere but nowhere. If you looked hard enough in the late 1990s or early 2000s in a cabinet or a drawer, they were there. And the book was probably delivered to your front door. Perhaps you even flipped through water-logged yellow pages at some point.

Here's the real point. This payroll company was making its way into our part of Florida. Some reps who had left the company were falsely advertising with the company's name, with payroll as the service, but listed their cell phone numbers. The truth was that the people who looked for payroll providers came into this yellow pages book and looked for a provider. They were buyers of payroll services. I saw that my company was being threatened by former employees who were mischievously using the cover of the company name, but then were getting calls and selling for a competitor. I took it upon myself to call the yellow pages company, place a correction in the book, and run the ads, as if that were a good idea to generate leads. It generated a few here and there—nothing earth changing. But it was earth changing that I made these "executive" decisions to place ads, and it led to my demise. The day they called me in, they had the freshly printed yellow pages that had been delivered to thousands of cabinets and I had dared to put my cell number in it. The leadership immediately wanted to own my personal cell number. I didn't budge. So here's what happened in a better, more visual way.

I got called into the district manager's office. I walked in. I turned the corner into the office, and the regional manager was in one chair facing the district manager's desk. I was asked to sit in the other chair. They both had this blank stare, both wearing cheap suits. Both had dark hair, and they appeared to be Italian/Middle Eastern. They had a sort of cult-like protectionism of each other's fiefdom. It was a political hierarchical thing with this company, kind of like the fashion industry—one day you're in, the next day you could be out. So I sat down and asked what I was in there for. They pointed to the yellow pages. The district leader opened to a page that was dog eared and asked, "How did you place this ad?" I told them the story of protecting the company, ensuring that any leads went to us. They believed that the reason I was selling ten times more than everyone else is that I somehow rigged the system and hijacked all of the leads from the yellow pages. They wanted the leads to flow into an 800 number so they could be divided up among the sales teams.

The reality was that there were very few calls that came through, and most of the leads sucked anyway. The real work I was doing was hard—pounding the pavement, hitting the bricks, and making the damn calls. That was how to make it in sales. So they asked me to hand over my phone and sign my personal number over to the company. I looked at them both as if they were crazy. They said I had two choices: give them my personal cell phone number or get fired. I took the second choice.

So that was it—quick and painless. I walked back toward my desk, where I was then directed to the door of the building. I couldn't get my notes or notepads, nothing. I was then escorted to my company car. I had to hand over the keys. A team of managers stripped the car, handed me the baby stroller from the back, and filled my pocket with change from the console. They then asked for the keys to the office. It was like being stripped of a career instantly. It's a good test of pride and an even better lesson in building character. It was a soul search.

As the cheap suits re-entered the building, I dialed up my Nokia and got a taxi. Apps and Uber didn't exist yet. As I rode in the taxi to my house, I thought about my wife, my toddler son, and my family. I knew what I was going to do next. As the taxi rolled up in front of my house, I exited and slowly walked to the front door. I entered. My wife came up to me, not realizing anything was wrong. I had not called her on purpose. She was glowing with happiness, the love of my life. She was mom of our toddler, and we had just bought a new house. She was still working at this point, and our daughters (my stepdaughters) were still in school. I held the news in pretty well that I had been fired, but I eventually let her know. At the same time, as I was downloading my mind in my home office, my two-year-old son handed me a note. It read, "Daddy, I am going to be a big brother." My wife was pregnant with another child, and I had been freshly fired. It was a bottom moment to remember. We always talk about it today. If something doesn't kill you, it makes you stronger. That is a true statement.

Fast forward to my first day in the insurance business. I was still doing photography on nights and weekends. It took years to rebuild the professional side of my career. But it clicked with me, and five years later, I became a partner in the company. In 2009, I sold the photography business. My focus was on group insurance products in the employee benefits industry. That was where it hit me. The passion emerged to help people through the placement of products to truly change lives. The products saved people from financial disaster caused from healthcare-related catastrophes.

Zoom forward another nearly nine years, and I had the makings of a phenomenal career. I learned a tremendous amount in this business. But it was time for me to go. I was motivated to start my own company and to be my own boss. The insurance agency I had worked for had filled its cup to capacity, but it wasn't enough for me. The people who were at the top were exhausted and wanted to hand over the keys to someone else. They would remain for the proper amount of time and then catch the next boat to the sunset. Though this sounded appealing and would mean greater financial impact, there were other details of the process that really bothered my soul. I was again itching to go out on my own. I knew I could do it, and now was the time. I remember the exact moment that I went to one of the most respected men in the business and tendered my resignation. He understood and acknowledged my interest to go for it. I knew he would be feeling that way. I learned a lot from him, but I wanted more. After thirteen years, it was a done deal.

The fire inside of me was ready. I worked from my home first. I created a new way to help people without the burden of insurance intermediaries. I did what I could to feed my family, get up every, day, and do what I loved, to serve others.

Through failures and successes, brick by brick, I built my own brand and my own companies, doing it all my way. As of the writing of this book, we celebrated a 400 percent growth since last year. After three years, we now have seven full-time employees and hundreds of employers who count on us for procurement of healthcare. There are two companies. One is a full-service employee benefits brokerage firm. The other is a software platform for medical companies to help thousands of people all over the country join membership-based medicine. Both have had tremendous growth. They are very different but critically important verticals of healthcare.

The silver lining of it all was that my progress in less than three years was equal to the sum of all my efforts in thirteen years put together from where I was before. My question is, why didn't I do this before? You have to live and learn. Nothing is a perfect roadmap, and I take every day as a gift. But ultimately, if you have the grit to go out on your own, at the highest risk, it will be worth it. In looking back, I don't regret anything. I think it all happened for a reason. I think it was all planned for me to be challenged, learn, challenge myself, break through unknowns, test new heights, and find new successes from failures along the way.

Despite all of this success, I put myself into over-drive, with fifteen- to eighteen-hour days. I wasn't watching my diet. I was eating more than I was burning. I was literally at the highest weight I had ever been at nearly 273 pounds. I wasn't getting more than five or six hours of sleep a night. I wasn't taking the time to spend with family on the weekends. I was always chasing the next deal. This was how I was engineering myself for an even greater failure. My body was vulnerable and I didn't see the opening to the unknown.

I was hitting the occasional CrossFit or Orange Theory Fitness class, but nutrition was all over the place. I wasn't eating enough of the right foods and not drinking enough water. I consumed too many sweets. My body was waiting for something to come by and sweep me off balance. I had no idea where this was going to take me.

3

The Annual Physical

I T'S A WIDELY known fact that we should get an annual physical. I had been consistent on this for years. My doctor kept phenomenal records that he and I could compare from year to year. There were usually no abnormal findings—just the same talk about BMI, diet, exercise choices, what would happen if I didn't exercise, etc. My typical routine for fitness was very inconsistent. I had joined different gyms from Crossfit to Orange Theory Fitness. Sometimes I would run at home. Often times, periods would go by when I wouldn't be doing anything.

I had no pre-existing conditions. I did have chickenpox when I was little, and then I had a small encounter with shingles that went away in my thirties. My blood work showed that I am ANA titer positive, which just means I have speckled red blood cells. I asked the doctors if this had anything to do with COVID-19 susceptibility, and they said there were no known tests about this. The ANA titer positive condition really is somewhat common, and in the majority of cases, there are no symptoms or any disease related to it. The other odd thing is that I am severely allergic to poison ivy. I'm not sure if that has anything to do with susceptibility to COVID-19, but I could literally brush against poison ivy and be covered within twenty-four hours. This sucks for someone who loves to do yard work and be outside.

Prior to getting COVID-19, my latest blood work showed that I had super low Vitamin D. My blood type is O positive. I would describe myself at that point as overweight, about 273 pounds, six feet one inch in height. I've always had lean athletic legs, but my waistline floated between thirty-four and forty-two inches, up, down, up, down. I actually had a wardrobe where I knew how I felt and which clothes to wear because I bounced up and down so much.

4

The Downward Spiral of COVID-19 and the Freestanding Emergency Room

THE SYMPTOMS STARTED as a normal annual sinusitis. I live in the tropical climate of Naples, Florida, where it's always warm and enjoyable. Once a year I seem to have my bout with sinusitis pain and stuffed nose. Usually when this happens, I will visit a walk-in clinic near my house. This time, the sinusitis set in. The magnitude of migraine-like pain was heavy. The nasal passages began to clog. This was the sign that a visit to the walk-in was necessary. I drove to the walk-in clinic, and luckily nobody else was in the waiting room. I was figuring at this point that I would see the doctor and get the typical run of steroids and antibiotics. In a few days, everything would be cleaned out and I would be ready to go. Boy, was I wrong.

The nurse called my name and led me back to the freshly painted patient room. She did the typical triage, performed a temperature check, verified my name and date of birth, and handled a few vitals. She asked what brought me in, and I began to explain that I was there for the typical annual sinusitis. She wrote down a few things and told me the doctor would be in.

Sitting there, I was thinking about how I couldn't wait to get back home, to get the steroids on board and the antibiotics cooking, and to recover quickly. I had a million things to get done.

The doctor entered. He listened to my chest and told me he thought it was the typical sinusitis similar to my history chart reflected each year prior. He asked me if I had ever seen an ear, nose, and throat specialist and gave me a recommendation to do so because of recurring sinusitis each year. As I always do, I ignored the advice.

As a precautionary measure, the doctor pulled out a long, irritating, Q-tip looking swab and told me it needed to go into my sinus cavity to detect the potential presence of COVID-19. At first, I didn't want to agree because I had presented with a sinus infection, so the thought of getting a long Q-tip up my nose to tickle my brain was not on my bucket list. Regardless, it happened, and it was horribly uncomfortable. This was before the instant COVID-19 tests, so I was given the paperwork and told the results would be available on my app related to the national lab where the walk-in clinic sent the test swab of my sinuses.

It was the end of the day on a Tuesday, and I went home. It had been a very long day and I was ready to settle down for a long weekend. I drove by the pharmacy and picked up the steroids and antibiotics. At home, I poured a nice large glass of water and took down the first group of steroid pills as well as the first antibiotic. It was a good evening of sleep and rest. I thought I'd awake to a fresh start, ahead of the sinusitis, ready to press forward into a new day.

As the weekend got closer, symptoms began to worsen. Migraine headaches kicked in as if someone were hitting the Liberty Bell around my head. I began to run a mild fever of 99 to 101. By the next day, I began experiencing random areas of muscle pain—my calves, my quads, the top of my feet, and the top of my hands. These symptoms were throwing me off completely. I had never experienced pain like this.

My sinusitis began to worsen. It seemed that my chest was beginning to get congested. As I breathed out, my chest made an odd wheezing noise that was light to begin with. I started a short, dry, hacky type of cough. I usually never coughed while I was sick. This was all throwing me off. The pain continued in the leg and arm muscles. The headaches were unbearable. I began to hack up dark phlegm, which wasn't too out of the ordinary with sinusitis.

The night was horrible. I tried to sleep, but I could not. I broke into massive cold chills, then I was hot, and then I was back to awful cold chills. I was sweating in my side of the bed so bad it felt like I would slap the puddle of wetness. Something was really awful about this. I kept going back and forth to the bathroom, and now diarrhea began. I started to think that maybe I had come down with the flu. It had crossed my mind that maybe this was COVID-19, because I had done research, and many of the symptoms I was experiencing could have been the dreaded virus.

I kept checking my results via the national laboratory's smartphone app. The results were in! I was positive for COVID-19. It all set in at that moment. Why was I having so many symptoms when I had no pre-existing conditions? Maybe I caught it at the local grocery store, the gym, or a national retailer; maybe I got it from a co-worker at one of my offices. I had no way to know.

At this point, I started to lose my sense of smell and sense of taste. I was literally exhausted. On one of my final journeys to the bathroom, I fell to my knees and violently vomited. I felt as if I were dying. Why was this happening to me? The greenish phlegm had now converted to a light colored bloody substance that I was coughing up, and it was beginning to hurt when I coughed. My daughter brought a pulse oximeter to the house. At first, the pulse oximeter was at 95. It wasn't long before it was consistently between 91 and 93 and declining. My wife urged me to call my primary care doctor.

I got my primary care doctor on the phone and ran through the events unfolding. He urged me to go to the freestanding emergency room just about a mile from my house to get a chest x-ray. At that point, I was still coherent enough to drive. Being young was probably a big help, but COVID-19 was defeating me.

I mustered up the energy to drive myself to the freestanding emergency room. I proceeded to the doors, which slid open automatically. I walked to the front desk, all masked up. I told them I was COVID-19 positive and I was experiencing horrible symptoms. I also mentioned that my primary care doctor sent me via his recommendation.

To my surprise, a nurse appeared and escorted me back to an isolated unit. I lay down on the hospital bed and began to explain to her what was going on. She asked me lots of questions, took my vitals, and told me the doctor would be right in.

I arrived to the freestanding emergency room extremely thirsty. I didn't like drinking water and probably was severely dehydrated from the symptoms I had been experiencing all day leading up to this medical visit.

The doctor arrived and introduced himself. He brought some sort of medical trainee/assistant in with him to observe. I felt that it was my luck that I was the patient for the trainee, but I guessed it really didn't matter. The doctor asked me about my symptoms. I explained the whole story from the start of the sinusitis, to the urgent care visit, to the horrible night before. I then explained that my primary care doctor asked me to request a chest x-ray. The emergency doctor said that he didn't take advice from primary care doctors and he would treat me according to his protocols. I wasn't sure what the hell that meant. He disappeared as quickly as he had entered. I realized that I was not the only patient.

A nurse appeared and began to attempt to draw blood. I told the nurse that my veins were small in my arms and were usually a tough stick. Sure enough, she learned this herself, and I got stuck about a dozen times until she finally inserted the needle into my vein. Unfortunately, it pulled just enough blood then stopped. I urged the nurse to get me a large cup of water and give it a few minutes for me to hydrate. Meanwhile, the nurse was making snide comments about her job and wasn't very pleasant at all. If you asked me, I'd say she hated her job. I was so glad I got her for a nurse—just my luck. It was the same feeling as getting behind someone in the grocery line who would suddenly get a declined card and had no other method of payment, or even worse, would whip out two hundred coupons. The nurse was almost pissed that my veins weren't making her job easier. She kept refusing my request for ice water. Finally, I asked for the doctor, and he agreed to let me have water. Twenty minutes later, my arm was giving enough blood to save an entire community. A special ops vein team emerged on the scene and planted an IV into my arm, where they start pumping me with fluids, steroids, and I believe antibiotics. This was such a great start to my healthcare system experience.

The nurse exited with the full vials of blood. The team members dimmed the lights and let me know that they would be back to me as soon as possible. The noises echoed into my isolated room. I clearly heard the conversations at the nurses' station. I heard the nurses bickering about their jobs, gossiping about patients, and even saying that they were irritated with one specific elderly COVID-19 patient who kept pressing the call-nurse button. As the noise rang, the little old lady was made fun of and the nurses kept saying, "Ignore it; it's her again." What did they think of me? I was a 43-year-old guy with "mild" symptoms. Maybe they weren't taking me seriously at all. I literally lay there in my jeans and waited. It was so cold in my room, you could hang meat market products there. I got up and found some blankets that I curled around my legs and up to my chin. I kept coughing and producing blood into the ice water cup and into the trash can near my bed. I was in and out of sleep. I kept looking at the clock and was losing track of time.

The noise of the sliding door meant that the nurse entered my room. She asked me to drink a full cup of a water-like substance that would be required for me to have a scan. After what felt like hours going by, a radiology tech entered my room. She had the typical COVID-19 garb on. She was masked up and was wearing a hazmat-type suit and a plastic shield over her face. She was so muffled I couldn't even understand what she was saying. All I knew was that I was transferred to another bed and would be moved to a room where I was going to an x-ray machine. I guessed I was getting the chest x-ray after all. I followed the instructions of the machine, which moved me in and out. The radiology tech was saying things, but I still had no idea what she was saying. It was like hearing someone yell through a thick blanket on the other side of bulletproof thick glass. At that point, the scanning was over and I was returned to the original room. I began to drink more ice water, which felt great in my throat, and occasionally I'd spit more bloody phlegm into the trash can or cup near my hospital bed. I had no idea what was next, and it hurt when I coughed. The pulse oximeter in the hospital was indicating that I was at 92 to 95 up and down.

The emergency room doctor appeared again and said he was going to release me to go home because I appeared to have relatively mild symptoms and I was young and resilient enough to knock this as long as I stayed home, took precautions, drank fluids, and maintained quarantine. I asked him about how I was still spitting up blood. He said it was expected with sinusitis and was somewhat normal. I believed him because he was the medical doctor. He gave me prescription for another round of steroids and some antibiotics to take over seven days. A nurse came in and escorted me back to the parking lot via the automatic sliding doors at the rear of the emergency room. The slow walk to the car didn't seem right. Maybe I would go home and this would be it in a few days. I wasn't sure what was going through my head.

That night at home was the most horrible night of my life. Taking the emergency room doctor's recommendation, I went home and lay in bed. My fever began to spike again. I had zero appetite. My energy was depleted. I kept drinking as much water as I could at that point. The pulse oximeter was now staying in the low 90s—in the 91 to 92 range. My wife was concerned. My breathing was getting worse, my chest hurt, my head hurt, everything hurt. I literally went through the night getting up every ten to fifteen minutes to walk around. I kept feeling worse and worse. I had no sleep at all, and then morning came. My pulse oximeter reading was consistently now in the 88 to 90 range. I felt horrible beyond explanation. I cried. I cried in my wife's arms, wondering why this was happening to me. I made my kids cry, which I didn't want to do. Maybe this was my time to go. Maybe this was the end. Why in the hell was this happening to me?

I called my primary care doctor again. I gave him my explanation about the horrible experience at the freestanding emergency room. This primary care doctor is very special. He has connections with our local community hospital in our town. He told me to go straight to the main hospital, where he told me they would be waiting for me at the emergency room. My wife packed a bag for me full of clothes, a charger for my phone, and some other necessities. I cried in our kitchen to her that I wanted to make it through this. My three kids surrounded me while my wife and I embraced, and the kids all put their arms around us. This was an intense moment. Was this going to get worse for me? Was I to return from the hospital? Was this going to be the last time I was to see my kids and my wife? I remember the sound of the door closing as I walked outside.

5

The Hospital

M Y DAUGHTER WAS driving me directly to the hospital. I had my mask on and I was staring out the passenger window. There wasn't much conversation—just fear. I felt cold chills and pain in my legs. Nothing but ill feelings came over me. I was still coughing up blood; it was just redder now. I had no idea what was going to happen from there.

Exhausted and having trouble getting a full breath, I arrived at the emergency room entrance, where I was met by a nurse who knew I was coming. My primary care doctor had called and made arrangements with the hospital. The nurse who checked me in was very sweet. She listened as I told her my challenges from the freestanding emergency room to why I was now in the hospital. She told me about her mild COVID-19 experience, and she was thankful about how lucky she was. I got checked in. The nurse checked my vitals and strapped on my identifying bracelets. I was now escorted to the emergency room, to the isolation unit where all of the other COVID patients were. I felt awful because I could see through the glass windows to the older patients who were struggling to breathe and dealing with much more awful conditions on top of the COVID-19 symptoms. Many would be moved to ventilators and some wouldn't make it out or ever see their families again. The fear was overwhelming.

I landed in a hospital bed, and as expected, I waited. In a fairly short time, an emergency room doctor arrived. He was super high energy. He asked me to put a pulse oximeter onto my finger. He asked me to follow him into the hallway, and I followed him for a few laps around the emergency room hallways. We then ended up back at the room. He looked at me and noticed my color wasn't quite right and my oxygen saturation level was still barely 90 percent even after a quick jog-like lap or two around the emergency department. Something still wasn't right, and I was still spitting up blood, which seemed to keep getting darker red, from light speckled to dark red. The doctor had a plan. He told me about the protocols that the hospital worked with on COVID patients. He wanted to order up some radiology work, more specifically a CT scan of my lungs. He wanted to start IV fluids for steroids and antibiotics. He also ordered some oxygen, which was a first for me ever in my life to have a cannula in my nose pushing oxygen in. At this point, I was getting only about a liter, and it was maintaining my levels closer to 95 to 98 percent. All I could think about was how my mother-in-law felt just barely a year before when she was in the hospital.

I was whisked away again to the radiology department. This was a similar routine to the freestanding emergency room, but I felt better that I was at the main hospital. Part of me wondered if that actually mattered or not. Everyone was masked up looking as if they were in hazmat suits. Nobody was talking, but short instructions from the machine told me when to breathe in and out. It all went by so fast. I was back in the room again, hooked back up to the IVs. I waited. The clock rolled by. The doctor entered and told me that I had bi-lateral pneumonia and my lungs were in pretty bad shape. The doctor said my lungs were typical COVID-19 looking lungs but also full of fluid. He proceeded to tell me that my liver was having problems and something about my arterial blood gas numbers were not adequate. He decided to admit me to the hospital. I wasn't sure whether I should feel relieved or doomed. Maybe this doctor actually understood me.

After hours of waiting, I got the news that I would be transported from the busy emergency department up to a room. I was rolled up to the floor of patients like me who were younger and did not have pre-existing conditions. I was settled into my room, again in isolation. I would hear from the nurses through the speaker and would have occasional visits from nurses who were checking my vitals and adjusting my oxygen.

In the hospital room, far up on a high level in the hospital, I was connected to the IVs where the physicians began to administer high doses of steroids and antibiotics. The physician who was assigned to me said that my case was pretty bad and that he was going to order that I be given Remdisivir (I called it the Trump drug) and I would receive five days of doses via IV. At this point, it overwhelmed me that I was going to be getting more IV-administered medications. I was trapped in this hospital for days to come with no family allowed to see me and having very little human interaction. Being a type A personality who loves people, this was a challenge.

My life, family, work, schedule—everything was ripped away and came to an abrupt stop. What about all of my appointments, my proposals, and the open enrollment meetings to conduct for new benefit customers? There was nothing I could do about it. At that point, I still felt awful. I had headaches, and I experienced body aches in my calves, quads, and lower back. I had no sense of smell. I was confined to the hospital bed.

The lower back pain was excruciating. It seemed that once I got positioned to a comfortable height and found warmth with blankets, someone entered to take my vitals. I never felt fully rested. The doctor told me that the lower back pain was from my bi-lateral lung infections. It literally felt like someone had been using my lower back for a punching bag over and over. The doctor showed me what to do. He showed me how to stretch specifically to help the pains. He recommended drinking gallons of water. I probably annoyed the nurse asking for water all day long. I drank a lot of it. On most visits, the nurse would bring me five or more cups of water without ice.

The doctor also recommended that when I lay in the bed, I should rotate to promote healing as the antibiotics set in, as well as the steroids and the Remdisivir. I religiously rotated and lay prone on the bed. I never even heard the word "prone" before. It was basically crossing my arms and lying face down on my stomach. It was not comfortable. The first night was horrible. I was constantly getting up to spit out blood and was producing phlegm from my lungs. I also had to pee constantly due to the tremendous amount of water.

The silver lining in all of this was that the food in the hospital was actually great. Three solid meals arrived every day, and they provided excellent nutrition for healing. With each day, my doctor lowered the amount of oxygen I needed. The nutrition department was always on point. They called me, took my orders, brought up the food, and came to take it away when I was done. These were fearless people amidst the pandemic, fully exposing themselves to COVID-19, just to make sure that the patients were eating properly. They were the unsung heroes of the pandemic, like many others.

6

Faith Experience

L ET ME FIRST plant an important disclaimer to
this section. While I can recount every event that
happened, I know there are people who may judge this as
complete "COVID brain," and there are others who may
judge this as a genuine faith experience or divine inter-
vention. I am inclined to think that parts of my experiences were illusions created by my swollen brain. I now
see these events as incredible experiences, none of which
hurt me or anyone else, and they have helped me have a
closer faith in God. More importantly, the whole experience of COVID-19 has brought me closer to myself, and
it has given me an inner appreciation for life.

When I got home from the hospital, I had finished
my fifth day of Remdisivir and a big IV dosage of
Dexamethasone and antibiotics. The hospital had also
been giving me high doses of vitamins. I hadn't really
ever taken vitamins consistently before. The take-home
prescription was another course of Dexamethasone
in pill form, which I followed perfectly. I also had a
breathing device that allowed me to measure the volume
of my lungs when breathing in. I worked on that every
hour in the hospital as I got back off of oxygen assistance.

At home I was consistently hitting a 97, 98, or 99 percent oxygen rate, so I felt great with my progress. To this date, I have no idea what combination or what specific medication may have contributed to my experiences.

At home I decided right away that I was going to run, lose weight, take vitamins, and never let myself be vulnerable to COVID-19 or any coronavirus again. I started getting up at 4:30 A.M. every day and running some mornings five miles or more. I did thousands of sit-ups, sometimes in bed. My wife wasn't saying anything; she seemed to ignore everything I was doing.

I purchased an Elliptigo bicycle online. It is essentially an elliptical machine on a bike. I did a lot of research and thought this machine would be perfect for me to get out and get some natural sun-blessed Vitamin D on my skin. When the Elliptigo arrived, I assembled it in my kitchen and took it out for a journey. I fell in love with this immediately and planned to make a routine of Elliptigo rides as well as runs. This was in addition to the sit-ups in bed, sometimes counting past 100 to 150 at a time.

I had flexibility as I never had in my life. I could literally stand up and put my hand flat on the ground, palms down, whereas before COVID-19, I could touch my toes, but it hurt. I didn't really understand why my flexibility was so incredible, better than it had ever been in my whole life. I shrugged it off and figured steroids were the reason. I took full advantage of this by working out. When I ran, I was sustaining seven- to eight-minute miles, which was rare for me. I hadn't done that in decades. One morning, I was running at full pace and ran up an embankment near the entrance to a community. I felt my legs stretch as they never had before. I was later told that supposedly I was bending my legs and that I wasn't really touching the ground with the entire bottom of my feet. I knew something was up because I really didn't have that kind of flexibility before COVID.

One the first morning, I ran to St. Agnes Catholic Church, which is where the first experience happened. I parked my Elliptigo and walked onto the church campus. I went over to the memorial wall where my grandparents', my great aunt's, and my uncle's wife's sister's cremains are stored behind personalized plaques where their names and their years of birth and death are engraved in granite.

Having remembered my prayers ever since my last Mass nearly twenty-seven years before in Catholic school, I placed my hand over my grandparents' plaque and said a "Hail Mary" prayer. I then did the same for my great aunt and my uncle's wife's sister. As I walked away, I felt a pull to the wall and literally heard all of the other people who were memorialized in the same wall asking me why I didn't bless them. I was shocked and looked around, but I didn't see anyone else nearby. I thought this couldn't be happening. I slowly stepped backward to a stone bench that had been donated to the church. I sat on the bench and positioned my hand from a distance so that when I raised my hand, it appeared to cover the entire wall. I then said a "Hail Mary" prayer. As I finished the prayer, the wall went silent. I was overwhelmed and thought to myself, *Did this just happen?*

I returned to the memorial wall many days thereafter, blessing the memorials of my relatives and thinking about everything. One morning, I ran into a lady at the wall and asked about her relative. She told me she had lost her husband. She told me about his life and how they were in love. She told me he died of cancer. I told her that her husband loved her so much and that he was safe in heaven. She cried openly and thanked me for the sentiments. It was a beautiful moment to share with her.

I walked away from the memorial wall on that first day and turned the corner to head back to my Elliptigo. I came face to face with a large life-sized statue of St. Agnes. When I made contact with the statue, the eyes were bulging at me. It made me feel as if she were amazed to see me and that she knew I could see her but she couldn't believe it. I went to the front of the statue, knelt before it, and said a "Hail Mary" prayer. I then heard a voice from the statue as I looked down in prayer. I assumed it was the voice of St. Agnes telling me about forty angels who assist her in the protection of this particular church and who are the protectors of churches. At that moment, I noticed something wasn't right on church's façade. There seemed to be a construction defect issue. I felt that it was somehow my calling to help the church make it right. I found out that the façade was being redone and rebuilt because the construction was damaged. I was destined to figure out how I could help. I donated treasures from my business to the church, specifically to the renovation and construction fund. I also found out that the church was short in its budget to fix the façade and it was taking longer than expected. Maybe St. Agnes was trying to tell me that the church needed my help. Or maybe it was a total coincidence.

After I had a moment with the St. Agnes statue, I walked to the outside stations of the cross. It immediately came to my memory from when I was a little boy of how we used to do the stations of the cross. I decided to stop at each granite stone that represented each station, say a prayer, and feel closer to my faith. I started down each station. When I got to the station where Jesus fell, I heard a voice telling me that the stone carving wasn't accurate in its depiction. The voice told me that there was one less person in the actual event from what was depicted by the artist. I didn't understand why I was being told specific things about the accuracy of the artistic carvings versus the actual events. Once I finished the stations of the cross, I went to visit a large display in granite of the Ten Commandments. I prayed and read all ten. I was in shock over my experiences and wondered why I was experiencing this.

Finally on this visit, I followed the path to what was a life-sized pure white beautiful statue of Jesus. The statue depicts Jesus probably in his early thirties, standing straight up with his hands held out from both sides. I had no idea what to expect and was a little scared as I rounded the corner and approached this statue. I felt an overwhelming sensation as I approached it. I initially thought maybe the statue would do something like the St. Agnes statue did, but it did not. I knelt before it and said the Lord's Prayer, thanking God for giving me a second chance at life after COVID-19. I then heard a voice telling me that Jesus had been on earth to spread the word of

God. It also came to me that I was given a responsibility through my role on earth to help others and to spread the message of faith. I heard this same voice telling me about how humankind on earth was really suffering and that darkness was overcoming the light on earth. I then was told that Jesus would always be with me to help me in my decision-making processes as my general counsel. I literally laughed out loud and was questioning myself the whole time while listening. I then heard a voice from Jesus telling me about his mistakes in how he spread the word of God, his Father.

He told me about how he made a mistake in spreading the word of God. The authoritative figures at the time did not like his way of messaging the faith of God. This contributed to his end on earth. He also told me he wished that during this time on earth through his human body, he wished that he had today's technology to spread the word of God. He told me that he wished he had an iPhone. I had a vision of a similar statue of Jesus, except in one hand was the sculpture of a granite iPhone. I thought that maybe I would sponsor putting a life-sized statue of Jesus at St. Agnes Church, but with Jesus holding an iPhone.

At this point, I left the church on my Elliptigo and headed home. I did not want to tell anyone what I had experienced as nobody would believe me, and I was questioning myself about the experience over and over again.

That night while I lay in bed, it hit me even harder. I started hearing voices and seeing people in my life who had died. I felt as if I could communicate with the dead and hear them clearly. I was very certain that there was a line of people who were my family members wanting to talk with me. I tried to peek into what I thought was heaven, but I was told that I couldn't see into heaven clearly and I wasn't allowed to. When I tried to look in, I could see a haze, behind which seemed to be the shapes of people walking. I started to think that I could antici-pate the thoughts of people all around me. I thought that I could read people's minds and also help them talk to people who had passed away. I felt that maybe I was a medium of some sort.

That evening, as I lay in bed, I felt that I was given the role of a prophet on earth under Jesus' command as my general counsel. I was told that I was surrounded by a protective sphere, and that evil and darkness could not come through. The protective sphere was thick and clear. I could breathe through it and it was transparent, but no human could see it. My mission was to spread light and goodness, which could not be killed by evil and darkness. I was told that at night, evil beings were going to try to come to me. I lay in bed and though I wasn't dreaming, or so I thought, I could see cloud-like shapes that appeared to be blue images flying away from me. From my eye straight ahead, the picture was solid black, but the blue images appearing as bursts of clouds were flying forward, like an endless symmetry of shapes going outward from my frontal lobe. During this process, I was also reciting Hail Mary prayers, one after another. I kept feeling that it was known that I was in this protective outer layer and I was being visited by evil beasts, though they could not get at me. I experienced this night after night as I lay in bed. I wasn't even sure if I even slept any of those nights after I arrived home following the hospital visits.

Tragically, in May of 2020, I lost my brother-in-law to an opioid addiction. He struggled for over twenty years with addictions. I had been part of my wife's family for seventeen years. After we lost my father-in-law five years ago, I was my mother-in-law's protector. We watched my brother-in-law make terrible decisions over many years, resulting in arrests, evictions, drug overdoses, and rehabilitation, all of which seemed to be a terrible repetitive cycle. He always seemed to perk back up with a chance of recovery around the holidays when he received gifts and money, and then he went back into his regular routine, with the same results each year. It was very tiring and emotionally draining on everyone in the family, especially me. We all loved him and hoped he would come out of the opioid issue, but he couldn't.

On one of the nights as I lay in bed, I was told how my brother-in-law, while he was living, made a deal with the devil. He asked the devil for the ability to survive deep, dark overdoses of opioid binges. He had been through at least fifteen near-death experiences with drugs, making it out of nearly every one of them. When he was at his worst stages, we would all wonder if he would make it out. My mother-in-law wondered for endless nights where he was, what he was doing, and how he was making it. She loved him so much as her only son and the younger of her two children. I talked her through thousands of hours of hope, faith, and love that he could make the right decisions and come out of this.

The deal that the devil made with my brother-in-law, so I heard, was that he would bring a child onto earth and in exchange, the devil would give my brother-in-law protection from death from opioid overdose. What my brother-in-law didn't know was that the devil also included invisible ink, which included his sister, my wife, in the deal. The deal required that my brother-in-law's evil spirit would reign inside my wife's body until I, as brother-in-law, got him out. And the devil wrote in the invisible ink that his wishes of no death due to opioids would not be granted, the devil would infect the child, and my brother-in-law would hang alive in purgatory for eternity, never to see his mother.

When I learned this, the next thing happened, which I still cannot shake as to whether this was real or not. Once I learned about my brother-in-law's deal with the devil, I looked over at my wife in bed while she was sleeping. I said to her, "You're coming out," referring to my brother-in-law's evil spirit. My wife turned to me with her eyes closed and said, "I am not fucking coming out." I kept repeating, "You are coming out," and she kept repeating, "No, I am not." It kept bothering me, and I continued to keep thinking that there was no way this was real, but the sheer feelings coming over me were terrifying. What if this was real? What was I supposed to do to get him out of her? I was told by a voice that I had to massage him out of her, and that he would be released at the bottom of her spine, on her lower back, into my hand. To accomplish this, I had to massage her hands, up her arms, down her shoulders, and then her feet up her legs, all to the same spot in the lower part of her back. I did this, and she didn't even wake. Once I did this long massage, there was a small bump protruding on her lower back, by the bottom of her spine. I got up out of bed and walked around to her side. I said a Hail Mary and cupped my hand over the spot. It hit me like a baseball pitch into my hand. I tightened my grip, and my long fingernails were hurting as they clutched into the palm of my hand. I had the evil spirit of my brother-in-law out of her body. She was still lying completely asleep.

I stood there in complete doubt, but had a feeling that I had just caught a bug and I didn't know what to do with it. In our bedroom is a stand-up mirror. I looked over at it and figured I could launch the evil spirit into the mirror. I wound up like a baseball pitcher and threw what I thought was the evil spirit into the mirror. The feeling that it bounced against the mirror and back into the palm of my hand was terrifying, that the evil spirit was back in my hand. I felt my palm pulsing and I was getting extremely sweaty.

The only thing I could do was walk outside and see if I something or someone would tell me what to do. I walked into our living room and opened our slider door. I decided that first I had to drown the evil spirit. I knelt down by our pool and held my fist underwater. As I looked down at it, it seemed that bubbles were coming out of my fist as if the water were boiling. I held it there until all of the bubbles stopped. It took a few minutes for the bubbles to stop from a boiling like state to just a few, then none. As I raised my fist out of the water, I heard a message that told me to take the evil spirit to the front and launch it into the black hole, straight up into the sky, and into the black hole, which is the door to hell, never for the evil spirit to return. I took this message and went to my front door and walked outside down my driveway.

As I looked up straight into the sky, it was cloudy. I raised my opposite hand into the sky and opened my hand, which made an opening in the clouds, like a dark black circle opening. With that, I looked around and saw nobody around. I launched my other hand and opened it up to send the evil spirit straight up into the black hole. As I released the evil spirit, my hand stayed in the same position, open and shaking and pushing all the way, until the evil spirit landed in the black hole. Once it had landed, I felt the release of pressure and my arm came down.

I attempted to explain this situation to my wife the next morning, but she didn't respond. She didn't even move or remember any of it.

I went back into the house and told my uncle, who was in our front room, what had just happened. I told him that I was going to get him first, but I knew I could handle it on my own. I later heard that he thought maybe I had accidentally hurt my wife or did something to someone else. He was worried about me the whole time. He and I have been very close for our entire relationship. During my COVID-induced experiences, my uncle hung in there with me. He was actually communicating with my mother and my siblings the whole time. He was concerned that maybe I had to go back to the hospital due to the way I was acting. He even went with me to the doctor's appointment, which was done via Zoom.

After I had spoken to my uncle, I went back to my bedroom. I was sweaty and had enormous energy, and

I was unable to sleep. I went to my computer and was playing around online. I had a certain feeling overwhelming me. As I looked over my shoulder, my wife's knee went up in the air, under the covers. I could hear my brother-in-law talking to me. But he spoke like he did when he was having his good times. He sounded younger, healthy, and vibrant. I got a message that his punishment for making a deal with the devil was that his good spirit would have to exist inside of his sister. It would help heal her from any future heart disease or any other issues she was going through. Once he accomplished this, he was allowed to rise into heaven to be with his mother for eternity.

As my wife's knee went up, it was as if a student were raising his hand. I said, "What is it?" He said, "I want to go see my mother." I told him that he wasn't allowed until he ensured that his sister was safe, happy, and healthy. I ignored him a few times. After I answered the first time, her knee went down. Then it went up again. I asked him what he wanted. He was acting super impatient and wanted to know when he could be with his mother. I told him that he had a required task, and until that was done, he wouldn't be let go. I assumed that I would be required to do the same process with his evil spirit, and that I would have to do this with his good spirit. The way it was left was that he was kept inside of her to protect her. His sister always protected him when he was little because the parents were never home and he wanted her to protect him, which was part of the deal with the devil. The only problem was that he didn't know the devil never makes deals that are good for anyone. It's always a one-sided deal, which also had been drafted with invisible ink.

I kept getting messages about history and the beginning of God's creation of the earth. I saw how God put people of all races onto the earth simultaneously. All races of people touched the earth, all at the same time. I saw how a man and woman in various places around the earth were placed onto the soil at the exact same time. It was like the scene from *The Shawshank Redemption* when Andy Dufresne touched the idea that the word "race" wasn't about skin color. It was about the race to maintain humankind. God designed humankind and required that humans work together to protect the earth. It was expected that the races across the earth would meet and mix together over millions of years. No natural event would destroy the earth during human existence; humans would either destroy themselves or live in unity to perpetuate into the future.

When the earth got out of control and darkness proceeded beyond the light, God had to intervene. He sent Jesus down as a man to sacrifice himself to remove all evil and give humankind a new fresh start. The design beyond that was that God would provide the earth with prophets, guided by Jesus. Jesus would infinitely be the general counsel of the prophets. He would guide them to make the right choices. The prophets had the responsibility to spread the light and help keep the darkness away from humankind while they were here on earth. Most of the prophets were not thought of as prophets. They became great leaders, and everyone they touched would follow them and listen to them. They had a genuine charismatic talent that God gave them to do amazing things. This incredible talent could never be learned by an ordinary person.

The problem with the prophets was that in many instances, they realized their power and sought fame for themselves, which led to their demise. Back to the very beginning of Egypt, God sent prophets. Jesus was the only Son of God, incarnate of the virgin Mary. There as a line of prophets before Jesus who knew about the creation of the earth. The prophets had infinite knowledge of humankind and were asked to spread the word of God. The problem was that the prophets were human and could think for themselves, often getting into massive problems, leading to their deaths, either self-inflicted or killed by others. I was also told that there are multiple prophets on earth at the same time with different missions to help people or for specific causes. I was feeling overwhelmed with a message that humans haven't found many of the written missing scrolls. The majority of them are buried under the sands of Egypt, miles beneath the surface.

In one of my businesses, the developers that I hired actually resided in Pakistan. I received an email letting me know the holiday schedule of when the developers weren't available. I did some research about these traditions I had never heard of, including the Pakistan holidays. Interestingly, they remarked about the prophets. One of the developers told me a story about a prophet who had gotten a message from God that he had to kill his only son. But before the prophet did so, God intervened and presented an animal for sacrifice instead of the prophet's son. I asked my developers about their belief in faith. They said that they questioned the actual faith meaning, but more intently learned from the lessons. So as a holiday to celebrate this event with their prophet, they raise an animal, such as a cow, and then in celebration of their faith, they slaughter the animal. But while some people may say that's cruel, the animal sacrifice provides food for the poor and many others. So the faith-based story about the prophet leads to an infinite greatness in helping others, which is a beautiful thing. This all stemmed from a prophet story that happened thousands of years ago.

I was given an explanation about the human body, and I thought I was experiencing how it is supposed to exist on earth. First, God's design was that lungs were to look like angel wings. This seems reasonable, given that lungs and wings are similar in shape. Secondly, the stomach was made into the shape of a waterskin that would hold water in ancient Egypt. Waterskins were carried across deserts. Humankind would be allowed to use up to 25 percent of a brain's potential. But in certain instances, humankind would accidentally tap into the potential above 25 percent. The prophets were allowed to have up to 75 percent brain utilization, which enabled them to see things others could not and to have knowledge greater than anyone else. Jesus' brain was enabled to 100 percent, which enabled him to be fully communicative with the other side and to release his abilities and powers.

I thought that food was disappearing on my tongue and evaporating into the roof of my mouth. I was eating specific fruits and vegetables, but they weren't going to my stomach; rather, they were evaporating into the top of my mouth, straight into brain food, which would supply the rest of my body. Many mornings, I sat and ate, thinking that strawberries disappeared in my mouth, into the top of my mouth, directly into my brain. I guess that brings new meaning to "brain food." I was convinced that the stomach was designed purely for water only. The body was designed to eat certain foods. Foods that are harmful wouldn't pass through the roof of the mouth, go down into the stomach, and make the body sick.

I wonder if there is a way that the body is supposed to consume food differently or more ideally for the human body to function. If we performed that process and consumed the right types of foods, it's clear that our bodies are healthier, but what is that perfect balance?

I thought that I was able to see into the future and see how humankind will be able to leave the earth ahead of the earth's destruction. A technology emerged allowing humans to breathe easier in space as well as travel faster. The technology had to do with a helmet that could self-produce oxygen, allowing humans to breathe in space. It almost looked like a clear Darth Vader helmet. Humankind actually would end up hopping from planet to planet. Essentially we would inhabit a moon, leaping from the moon to Mars, inhabiting Mars, then leaping from Mars to the next planet and so on, until humankind reaches the end of the galaxy. I was also told that we are not the only humans—that ours is just one of millions of planetary systems where humans like us exist.

These were all of the things that happened to me in the time following my COVID experience. I had been raised Catholic. It had been nearly twenty-seven years. To the moment as I write this book, I have not missed a Sunday since my COVID experience. The first time I missed was when I went to Tennessee with family after Christmas for our escape vacation. The second time was literally the day that my father lost his battle to cancer, although I brought in a priest from a local Catholic parish. He helped my father have a passage anointed with holy oil. My father was a dedicated man to his faith, and he deserved a proper passage. He's in a better place now. And through all of this experience, so am I.

I felt compelled to make sure my father had a proper passage. As he lay there in the hospice facility, I made sure he was able to tell all the family members that he loved them. And in turn, they could tell him that they loved him also. After that was completed, I successfully helped all of his children leave any judgment at the cross. He died knowing that all of his children loved him without judgment, and he could properly pass knowing that.

We don't know what happens for sure when someone dies, but the spirit and human container separate. I truly believe that the spirit goes to another place, which most refer to as heaven. Interestingly, I heard a priest recently talk about cremation. He said that when someone dies, the spirit passes on, but the human remains left on earth, which are usually cremated, should not be separated. So, he was referring to not putting cremains in a necklace, separate from where the remains are put for memoriam. I am not sure where it talks about that in the Bible, but it was interesting. It essentially infers that once our spiritual existence moves on, the container that is left can only be memorialized as a whole part, but not in separation. I suppose that is open to interpretation.

I am actually intrigued by the mysteries of faith. As a kid in Catholic school, I always questioned the existence of God. I think we all do at some point, whether we admit it or not. As a child, I was told what the stories were. I memorized prayers, and repeatedly I went to Mass, had faith-based classes, and through a self-fulfilling prophecy, I believed. But were the foundations of my beliefs truly solid enough for me to be a true believer? I think those of us who went to Catholic school can all relate. I came away from all of that as a true believer, but I stopped practicing after I left the area where I grew up. I think I always had a touch or thought process with God and faith. There were many times when I was down or sad about something. I naturally favored asking God for help. I think faith is a natural thing. There are those who deny it. There are also those who hide behind the cross. That's a whole other book.

At the same time, the deeper meaning of faith comes from more of an existential perspective on one angle. Why do we exist? Where did we come from? The biblical stories give humanity an explanation as to the existence of humankind, but how do we actually know? I think the answer lies in our own interpretation of faith, and whether we choose to believe or not. I am convinced that there are more believers than non-believers. I visited Long Island many times, and the old historic churches are an amazing thing to see. These churches go back hundreds of years and are scattered all the way up the Long Island towns. Of course, I realize that faith and religion have existed since the beginning of time. People spend lifetimes reading, researching, and trying to find the answers, facts, and explanations of it all.

7

Big Health Changes

THE AFTER EFFECT of my COVID experience created a new me that I hadn't seen or felt in years. The "COVID brain" faded, and I was back to normative neurological functions. The insane part is that I remember most of the experiences that happened while I was coming through the COVID recovery process.

I noticed that my fingernails grew out at a pace I had never had in my entire life. I had always been a nail biter, but somehow that stopped completely. I now have cloudy white nail beds, both fingers and toes. I never had that before. I was able to breathe better than I did before COVID, although that probably had to do with losing weight, which I've noticed before. I've always bounced from waist size 38 to 40 and back to 38 then back to 40. I actually was pacing at mile times that were harder for me to do. I found I had an improved breathing pattern and could sustain much longer distances running. My runs consist of 4.5 miles, and I follow them with four-to six-mile Elliptigo rides. I then enjoy a great breakfast consisting of fruits. I am trying to avoid high-sugar foods, although I have always had a sweet tooth, which my kids all inherited. The rare event that a bag of M&M's enters our house would be like honey to bees to our family. Even

67

if I hide the bag, somehow it slowly goes down, even if I don't have any.

I lost almost 34 pounds. Gained new energy and purpose. I reconnected with my faith. Somehow a higher being and power let me continue to have my feet on earth. I firmly believe in God, always have. I returned to church after having been at a Catholic Mass 27 years before prior while I was in Catholic school. The insane part was how dramatically different Mass was my last time versus how it was conducted now. I didn't initially understand how people can dress so unprofessionally in church. I didn't understand how certain things changed in church, such as specific rituals I remembered or traditional parts of Mass. How did all of these things change over a 27 year period. Almost baffled me. I felt like if the way people perceived church changed that much over a 27 period of time, how has Mass changed over hundreds of years or even thousands. What exactly is Mass supposed to be other than truly being thankful to God, praying for others and a community joining together in unified faith?

I am closer to my family members than I have ever been. When you go through a crisis, it's amazing how you see who would be there for you, no matter what. You also see who wouldn't be. While I was in the hospital, I realized who was asking about me the most. I could feel the genuine love that my family has for me and the fear that they might lose me. My wife had suffered tremendous losses over the last few years, losing her dad, mother, and brother. She only has me and our children left. Now she was distressed at the thought of also losing her husband.

The worst part of it was that she couldn't see me in the hospital, as there were no visitors at the time of COVID.

I think my experience also brought me closer to my brother. While I already regarded him with the highest respect and admiration, this COVID process made me realize that he would do anything for me, as I would for him. He was calling my wife, asking about me and concerned about my well being. I would have expected that, but he was clearly shaken by my challenge. I know that no matter what, my brother would always be there for me. I am lucky to have a sibling like that.

On a daily basis now, I take two tablets of zinc (50mg each). I also take magnesium, vitamin C, and vitamin D. I never took vitamins before, as I have never been a pill taker. I'm always trying to exercise, to eat the right things, to manage weight, and to steadily grow older while staying healthy. At least that's my plan. I am committed to seeing my primary care doctor at least once a year and am committed to routine exercise.

Getting natural full sun has been wonderful not only for my skin but also for my mind. I am less stressed and more rested than ever. I venture out for running, followed by Elliptigo riding. I love it. The deep breathing into my lungs is so important for my body. I can feel the deep open area of my mind, allowing me to think. It makes me think about the fact that my body can handle the exercise; it's the brain that stops us and defeats us. We must defeat our very own mindset and stay strong and not lose ground. We must not lose balance within ourselves. The more I run, the more I realize that it's the mind that tells me to stop, to give up, and to not run anymore.

My legs don't have a voice, but they do have a breaking point far beyond what my brain thinks they can handle. Pushing past our perceived limit is critical for success and in fitness. I do not proclaim to be a fitness expert by any means. I like to listen and read about self-proclaimed fitness experts, though. They all have different approaches.

I am conscious of needing significantly more quality sleep. I stop pushing myself too hard and listen to my body, as my wife says.

My goal is to lose around twenty more pounds and try to stay around 215 to 225. I still have a way to go. It's a battle of mindset versus just making it happen. I know that. I have to break through and make it happen.

8

Mission from the Heart

S O MANY HAVE asked, "What do you do for a day job?" I have always loved being in sales. A career in sales is an emotional roller coaster. I remember back to when I finished my undergraduate work in Salisbury, Maryland, at Salisbury State University. At the time, it was a satellite location of the University of Maryland. It is a great college. It was nestled in a small town and originated as a state teacher's college in the early 1900s. It has become a well-known college in Maryland. The town of Salisbury is a beautiful stop on the way out to Ocean City, Maryland. I was in between two separate schools, the business school and the philosophy house. I loved both.

At the time, I worked for an independent pharmacy. It was a big local pharmacy serving lower Delaware, the eastern shore of Maryland, and northeastern Virginia. I remember hearing we did more than two thousand prescriptions a day. I always saw the pharmaceutical reps coming and going who were talking to our pharmacists. The reps came in, wearing fancy suits and carrying briefcases. They were sharply dressed professionals who I started building a relationship with. That became a dream job.

The owner of the pharmacy developed a program that would be a tremendous asset to my educational career. The company reimbursed me for 75 percent of my tuition. I remember talking to the owner about my grades. The program required high performing grades to receive the reimbursement, and I never missed one. There was a genuine feeling at this pharmacy where I really got to know the customers. It was like a portal back in time when communities had a local store and the locals were loyal to it. I remember distinctly the customers who would drive up and we would know from memory what they wanted. We always had it 100 percent right. Many customers were older. Many of them have probably passed at this point, but back then, they loved the attention. It made their day and it probably was a major event for them to go to the pharmacy to pick up scripts and other items.

At one point, the pharmacy owner wanted to educate the front counter staff about vitamin knowledge. The owner was super sharp and had been in high rankings with a pharmaceutical company before getting into management at this pharmacy and eventually taking over as owner. He was educating us about the importance of certain vitamins related to medications that could diminish certain vitamins in the body. He knew we had relationships with the customers. I had been there for years and was a known face. He then incentivized us by telling us we could make $5.00 per vitamin bottle. It became a competition. The process was pretty cool. When we saw a customer who was taking a script that could very likely be lowering or depleting specific vitamins, we recommended it. And if the customer had more questions, we brought out the pharmacists, who were always happy to answer questions and provide advice. I remember most of the front counter clerks (mostly all college students) weren't really into selling these vitamins. I think I hit fifty bottles in one month before the owner shut down the program. The cool part was that I was really helping people.

9

New Mindset, New Me

THIS WHOLE EXPERIENCE gave me a new appreciation for life on earth. It has helped reinforce my "Why." We are servants on earth with a mission to help others. When I was suffering in the hospital wondering if it would get worse and wondering how my family was, I felt lost. I lay there in the hospital and reflected on everything—my family, my life, my choices, and my mission in life. The experience helped me see the reason for life and helped me draft a solid roadmap, more certain that ever. I have a mission to make sure that my children have successful paths. I have a solid marriage and I am deeply in love with my wife.

During my COVID experience, everything I had going on at the company level came to a hard stop. We had close to twenty companies through a combination of renewals, new deals done, and prospective deals, along with a tremendous amount of over-the-top service. I felt totally disconnected, yet all of it happened and it was done exactly how I would have wanted. COVID extracted me from my way of living and erased my old way of thinking. It changed my wiring for the better. My employees kept my companies going even without me.

It's a blessing that any CEO would want. The employees made it happen. They knew exactly what to do. They cared enough. I was so proud to have this team in place. It ended up being a team that I could build off of to create a legendary company driving a mission from the heart. To truly help people is a magnet for success.

I truly want to see the best in others and watch them rise up. The highest professional achievement for me is to help an employee completely transform into something that they never thought could be possible. People want to have a purpose in both their personal and professional lives. If we can give people a true professional purpose, then they will work with a true passion to serve others. When someone crosses what they thought was their own threshold or stopping point, they want more. Creating a fire in someone that was never lit before is so gratifying. Growing a company isn't about just the revenue and the money. It's about building a place where people can grow personally and professionally. The more enjoyable the environment, the more people can grow and the more they will want to push the ship forward. They may even love working there so much that they have new ideas, and that helps the company charter into places it couldn't have without the talented minds. Scaling a company isn't possible without talented minds coming together.

The employees pressed the companies forward in my absence. They jumped into the work at hand, closed deals, finished tasks that I had opened, and made things go without me. The team humbles me every day. I am honored to work with people who aren't there just for themselves, but they are there to take care of others. We give gifts of our intellectual talent to others, and our customers see that as solid value, as they should. It's not company and customers, but it's people helping people and a company emerging from that. As I finish up this book, I am in the market for several new associates. Interviews are happening. The approach to the interviews has changed. I am looking for people who I can completely build into legends in their own right.

As I sat in the hospital recovering from COVID, I gazed out of the top floor hospital window watching the cars going down a busy road. I thought about all types of people, where they were going, what they were doing, why they were doing it, and why they were motivated. Were they heading to work, or were they heading to see a loved one? Were these people asleep or awake inside? Have they experienced a traumatic situation as I had? Were they aware of themselves and seeing their truest potential? I feel that the majority of people are just fulfilling mediocre things. I simply think that people follow a standard path. They would wish to work for someone like me to show them how to wake. My mission is multi-fold, both personally and professionally, and I have so much to give to others.

When I returned home, I wrote an article on LinkedIn. The power of social media is incredible. The article was not for sympathy, but it was to simply spread a message about my COVID experience. I got hundreds of direct messages from others who had a similar COVID experiences and wanted to share. It was humbling to hear the experiences of others and to share stories. I had over ten thousand views. My heart bleeds for the people who lost their lives or loved ones to this terrible virus. Many people had similar experiences to mine. Many did not have such a COVID brain experience, but I talked to some who did.

Without people, we have no company. Without people, my mission to help others is impossible. I know that I can achieve what I want to achieve only if I have people I can trust who believe in me.

I have to surround myself with others. It goes without saying that you can't be all things to all people. Scale is impossible alone. You have to be willing to let go of things and be confident in those you've chosen to be part of the mission. Build the right disciples to help fulfill the mission.

The very basis of this whole process has created a fire in me like never before to create companies that are legendary, capable of things nobody else could imagine. I wake up every day ready to help others and make major changes in healthcare. I've always been comfortable being uncomfortable, but this experience has brought a new light to perspectives. It's awakened me to what is real and authentic.

I encourage you to reconnect with your family members if you have gone off track. It doesn't matter how many years you've been disconnected. You should bury judgments and see the good in others. I wish all readers great health, peace, and huge success in finding your purpose and passion.